QUAKER CAVALIER

QUAKER CAVALIER

The Story of William Penn

by
JOYCE REASON

LUTTERWORTH PRESS
GUILDFORD, SURREY

First paperback edition 1984

ISBN 0 7188 2609 4

Copyright © 1965 Joyce Reason

PRINTED IN GREAT BRITAIN
BY EBENEZER BAYLIS AND SON, LTD.
THE TRINITY PRESS, WORCESTER, AND LONDON

CONTENTS

FOREWORD

The well-known picture by Benjamin West, of Penn's treaty with the Indians, shows him as grossly fat, and that is the idea most people have of his appearance. Now, this cannot have been true at that time, for it is recorded that after the ceremony Penn joined in the games of the young braves, and beat them!

Benjamin West was not born until twenty years after Penn died. He may possibly have talked with someone who knew the great man in his old age, when he was ill and unable to take exercise, and so did grow heavy.

In the excellent *Life of Penn* by Catharine Owens Peare there is a fine portrait of Penn as a young man, said to be the only authentic portrait of him ever made. The original seems to be unfortunately lost.

I

CAVALIER

TO thirteen-year-old Will Penn his father, Admiral William Penn, was a hero. As a little boy, the return of the dashing sailor from victories at sea had been an excitement and a glory; now, he was old enough to understand how difficult life could be for a man who had two great loyalties—to his country and to his king. In those days, the two did not always go together, for this was the year 1657, when Cromwell was Lord Protector and the young King Charles II was an exile overseas.

Admiral Penn had fought his country's battles on the sea, as he felt was his duty; but he still hoped for the return of the King, and there had been a dreadful time, three years ago, when Penn had lain for five weeks in the Tower under suspicion of treason and in peril of his life.

That was all over now, and the whole family— the Admiral, his Irish wife, Will, little five-year-old Peg and baby Dick were settled in Castle Macroom in the south of Ireland, where Penn had a grant of land. And here one evening, in the great gaunt hall of the castle, something happened which swelled Will's heart to bursting-point with love and reverence for his father.

The hall was full, for by the Admiral's orders all

the household servants—the grooms, the footmen, the waiting and chamber maids, Will's tutor, even the scullions and kitchen servants—were gathered to listen to, of all unexpected guests, a Quaker preacher! There had been a good deal of whispering and giggling, and some shocked exclamations, when it was known that the master had actually invited this queer vagabond to explain his extraordinary views in the castle itself. These Quakers —"Friends" they called themselves, Friends of the Truth—didn't believe in churches, it was said, or priests, or ordained ministers, or regular services. Could they be Christians at all? Their leader, somebody had heard, was a madman called George Fox, who wandered about the country preaching his ridiculous ideas, and very rightly being stoned and beaten and put in the stocks; and so had his followers—serve them right!

But the Admiral, good Churchman though he was, when he heard that the Quaker Thomas Loe had come into Ireland and was in that part of the country, would have no beating or imprisonment or setting in the stocks.

"Let us hear the man before judging him," he said.

So there they all sat, very well-behaved under the commanding eyes of their master in his great carved chair, his lady at his side and young Will on a stool close to him. Whether little Peg was allowed the treat we do not hear—if she was there she probably went to sleep.

8

Will fixed his dark earnest gaze on the strange figure in dusty, travel-worn garments, a broad hat on his head just as when he arrived. Very disrespectful, surely? Yet there was no insolence in the Quaker's manner, but a gentleness and sweetness that was most attractive. Then he began to speak.

Will had never heard anything like this before. The words came straight from the man's heart, every one ringing true, burning with a kind of quiet fire. He spoke of the love of God, and one felt that he knew and lived in that love. He spoke of the brotherhood of all men, and to Will not only his family and friends, not only the household gathered in the hall, but the soldiers of the garrison and the poor ragged Irish querns living in the desolate boggy wilderness of devastated Ireland, all became the children of God to be loved and reverenced. Then Loe spoke of that Inner Light, the Spirit of God in every man's heart, which, if only attended to, can guide through all the hardships, perplexities and sorrows of life, and give an unshakable peace and joy.

A memory came to Will, of himself as a little boy of ten, saying his prayers alone in his room, and suddenly having a lovely sense of light and happiness. Was this what Thomas Loe meant by the Inner Light?

The Quaker finished speaking. For a moment there was dead silence, then the quiet was broken by a loud sobbing. Will looked round to see who was making the noise—it was a negro servant of his father's, warm-hearted like most of his race, quite overcome by emotion. What would the Admiral say to this? Will turned his eyes to his father— amazement! Down the sailor's bronzed face the tears were streaming; he, too, had been touched to the heart.

If anyone had told Will then that in this moment of exquisite sympathy was the seed of a bitter estrangement from his loved father, how could he have believed them?

*　　*　　*

1660—Cromwell dead, the Commonwealth gone to pieces, the Penns back in London, King Charles II called to his throne. Admiral Penn, now openly on the side of the Royalists, had worked for the King's return, and was one of those who went on the *Naseby* to bring him home. Will was exultant when his father told him how, as he knelt before the tall dark King, Charles laid the flat of his sword on Penn's shoulder and bade him, "Rise up, Sir William Penn!" Bells and flowers, fountains running with wine, crowds yelling themselves hoarse at the grand procession, a gracious smile of recognition for Sir William from the King and the Duke of York, the King's brother, and another smile for the sturdy lad proudly presented by his father— was it any wonder that the memory of that evening at Macroom was for a while crowded out of Will's mind?

Sir William was given a post at the Admiralty under the Duke of York, for whom he had a special friendship. The world lay open before young Will —he could become anything he wished, but his father hoped he would become a diplomat, possibly an ambassador, perhaps even one of the King's ministers. Meanwhile, he was to go to Oxford. Then the trouble began.

Expelled! Not for roistering in the streets, not for duelling, or running after pretty ladies, or getting into debt, or any of the scrapes a handsome, wealthy young man of the world might get into, and be duly forgiven after a lecture and a period of rustication. No. What Will had done was not in the least amusing and was liable to wreck all his father's hopes for him. Attending lectures by Dr. John Owen, the Puritan, refusing to wear the student's gown; gathering for private prayer and worship with a group of sober "square-toed" students; generally behaving like a cursed young prig!

"Throwing away all your chances! After all I've done for you! Presenting you to the King and the Duke of York—and let me tell you the Duke looked very kindly on you. It isn't as though I hadn't warned you. But I've had enough of this—I've a good mind to lay my stick about your shoulders."

Which he did, and thoroughly, big lad as Will now was. But the boy steadily refused to "reform". The life at Oxford, he said, was dissolute, extravagant, ungodly, and he had had enough of it. Perhaps at this time he *was* a bit of a prig?

11

"Out of my house! I'll not harbour a Puritan in my family! Let your canting friends look after you —I've done with you."

But here Lady Penn interfered. This was too much.

"You can't mean it, husband! What will the poor boy do, at his age, without a home, without money—he's only a lad. He'll come round. He's seen nothing of the world yet. A good, steady boy at heart. And what will I do all alone if you go off on your travels in the King's service, and me with my eldest son lost to me? It's too much and I can't bear it. Sure it would be the death of me."

"But what's to be done with him?" Sir William wavered before his wife's pleading. "He can't return to Oxford."

"Let him go abroad for a while. With the grand introductions you can give him, he can see the French court, learn fine manners, make new friends—only give him a chance to see life and he'll drop all these crazy notions."

So to Paris went Will, to the glittering, extravagant court of Louis XIV, called the "Sun King".

*　*　*

Night in the Paris streets. A young cavalier pacing soberly between the tall gabled houses towards his lodging, his plumed hat and fine silks and ruffles contrasting oddly with his grave face. Will was deep in thought, so deep that he did not notice another cavalier of his acquaintance who swept off his hat in greeting. Suddenly he found himself confronted by a flushed angry face and a drawn sword.

"Sir, you have insulted me! I demand satisfaction!"

"Insulted you? Why, what have I done?" Will came out of his reverie bewildered.

"When I saluted you just now you ignored me!"

"Why, I am sorry, but the truth is I did not see you."

"You have insulted me. Honour must be maintained. Draw, or I call you coward!" And the fiery gentleman aimed a stroke at the Englishman.

But Will's sword was out, he had been well trained, and had a natural aptitude for sword-play. The ring of steel, a clash or two, and the Frenchman's sword flew out of his hand. He was at Will's mercy, and by the foolish laws of duelling he might be slain out of hand for the unprovoked assault. Will's unstained sword slid back into its sheath.

"Is the ceremony of raising a hat worth the life of a man?" he said, more to himself than to his adversary. "Is it worthy of a son of God, or of benefit to society, to kill for a point of honour?"

And he passed on, leaving his opponent dumbfounded.

*   *   *

Dublin Castle, six years after the return of Charles II, was like a little court. Cavaliers whose long curly wigs fell halfway down their backs, ladies whose jewels flashed and silken skirts rustled, danced to the sound of fiddles and flutes, gossiped and flirted or rode out hawking in gorgeous cavalcades. Here lived the Lord Lieutenant of Ireland, the Duke of Ormonde, as grand as the King himself; here was his eldest son, the Earl of Ossory, and many another fine young nobleman. And among them, as handsome as any, graceful, accomplished and friendly, moved young Will Penn, son of the Admiral, friend of the Duke of York, looked on kindly by the King. His years in France had given him poise and grace; a few terms studying law had sharpened his wits; with it all he had charming manners, was modest and unassuming. No wonder he was a favourite with everybody.

He was in Ireland on his father's business, looking after the estates which had been granted to Sir William by the King, and that business often brought him from the grey old castle near Cork to the little court in Dublin. He was there when startling news came out of Northern Ireland.

Mutiny! The garrison at Carrickfergus on Belfast Lough had rebelled! Now the young gallants must put off silks and laces and don buff coats. Musket and sword was the order of the day. Will Penn, trained to arms as a matter of course, offered his services to the Earl of Arran, and was given command of a company of foot soldiers. Northward they rode, a grim band of warriors, and Will found to his pleasure that he could handle his men easily and win their respect. He knew it was going to be no pleasure party.

They came in sight of the stern fortress, strongly built for defence, bristling with rebel soldiers, skilled in arms. Will smelled the bitter smoke of gunpowder, heard the roar of cannon, saw men fall about him as the fire was returned. He held his men steady.

At last the wall was breached. "Forward, men! Show what you can do!" Will rode with his men—dismounted—took his part in the bitter hand-to-hand fighting, foremost and fearless, until what were left of the mutineers threw down their arms and surrendered.

"There's the making of a first-rate officer in that young man," said the Earl of Arran, and news of Will's exploits went to London and to Sir William, nursing a gouty foot at his home. Back in Dublin, the Duke of Ormonde received Will with congratulations.

"Your first taste of war, eh? Well, you bore yourself like a veteran. We could use you. Your father is captain of a company, of course, but I hear he is sick and can't take up his duties at present. How would you like to take his place? Do you think he would be willing to resign in your favour?"

"Why, your Grace——" Will was flushed and triumphant. "Surely your wish would be his—I'm honoured—I should be delighted—my Lord of Arran did speak of this at Carrickfergus."

"Then you are not unprepared. I will write to your father. Do you write likewise."

Will wrote an excited letter to the Admiral, in which his pride and pleasure were well mixed with the love and humility he bore towards his father. He was quite sure the answer would be "Yes"— how could the Admiral refuse the request of the Lord Lieutenant? So when his father's letter did come, it was rather a shock.

Sir William was certainly not going to give up his castle and his command to his son. The boy was far too young for such a responsibility. "I wish your youthful desires mayn't outrun your discretion," he wrote. He had other business for Will —the matter of the estates was not yet settled, and then he wanted him back in London. Though he did not say so, he had far more ambitious plans for his talented, beloved son than the command of a castle in Ireland.

Will, of course, was disappointed, but he submitted without a murmur, and devoted himself to the affairs of the estates. As his warlike excitement died down, he found that he was not really so disappointed after all. The time was not far off when he would be devoutly thankful to his father for preventing him from taking up a military career.

Little sister Peg was now fifteen, and going to be married. Not perhaps a great match, but a wealthy one, to a Yorkshire gentleman named Anthony Lowther. Will came home for the wedding, to a sad London, still mourning the Plague of the year before and the Great Fire which had left its buildings in ruins and its streets charred and black. The wedding was therefore a quiet one, just a family affair.

It was a happy family reunion—the last for many a year.

2

QUAKER

THE woman who kept the shop in the old walled city of Cork did not recognize the handsomely-dressed cavalier who bowed to her so gracefully, but she liked his warm smile.

"My name is William Penn," he introduced himself, "and I'm no stranger here. Years ago I lived with my father at Macroom Castle. This shop was kept by Friends, then, and I'm no stranger to Friends either, for my father once invited Thomas Loe to speak at the castle." He was silent for a moment and memories came flooding back. "Heigh-ho!" he sighed. "I would walk a hundred miles to hear Thomas Loe speak again!"

"Thou needst not walk so far, William Penn," replied the good woman, addressing him in the plain Quaker fashion. "There will be a meeting of Friends in this very town tomorrow, and Thomas Loe will be speaking. Thou hadst best stay overnight, and then thou canst hear him if thou means what thou says."

William had returned to Ireland after his sister's marriage, to look after his father's estates and to wait for an indication of what was to be his life's direction.

He was at the fork of the ways, just come to manhood, with great powers stirring in him of which he was only partly conscious. On the one hand, he could look for a brilliant career in his country's service, honour, riches, and power to do much good. The other path he could not see, yet when it opened, though he had no idea where it would lead him, he followed it without question, knowing that it was God's way for him.

Like most important things in life, it all came about so simply. He wanted new clothes, and rode into Cork to order some. When he was a boy at Macroom he had known Cork fairly well, and he remembered that there was a good tailor's shop kept by a Quaker. He inquired about it, and found to his pleasure that it was still there.

*　　*　　*

The soberly dressed Friends were not a little surprised next day, and some were a little nervous, when the plumed, bewigged cavalier, sword at side, stepped into their meeting. William himself must have felt rather conspicuous, but he sat down quietly and waited in the silence. The first speaker did not stir him much, but when Loe stood up, ten years older, marked by hardship and suffering, William felt all, and more, of the old warmth and attraction.

"There is a faith that overcometh the world," Loe began, "and there is a faith that is overcome by the world."

19

The words were like a searchlight turned on William's life. The way of worldly honour that seemed marked out for him was the way that would surely lead to the overcoming of his faith. In that heavenly illumination it no longer looked tempting —it was dry and empty and worthless. What was the other way, then?

William had seen in action the faith that overcomes the world. He had seen it in plague-stricken London, where, when many of the regular clergy fled, Quakers and other Dissenters moved about fearlessly, tending the sick and comforting the dying. He had heard of Quakers thrown into prison, refusing to give up their meetings, refusing to take an oath because to swear any oath at all was against their conscience. He had from time to time seen Quakers sitting in the stocks, jeered at and pelted with mud and rotten eggs, bearing it all with patient dignity. He had grieved for them, but at that time there had not seemed anything that he could do about it. Now, perhaps, the time had come to take sides, whatever the cost . . . suddenly he found that tears were streaming down his cheeks.

Loe finished and sat down. William wanted to say something, to express what was happening to him, but he did not know how to do it. Besides, he was no Quaker—yet. Had he a right to speak? Then an inner voice whispered, "How dost thou know but somebody may be reached by thy tears?"

William stood up, and all heads turned to look at the handsome, silent figure with the weeping eyes. Being Friends, they understood without any need for words. At the end of the meeting they gathered round him, made him welcome, invited him to their modest homes, and arranged that he should have a long talk with Thomas Loe.

Loe had so much to tell him, William had so many questions to ask. He learned more of George Fox the founder, who knew with a blazing certainty that God was with him anywhere, at any time, and His voice could be heard more clearly in the silence than through the words of any priest or service book. That was surely true for Fox and his followers, but William may have wondered, later if not at that time, whether all people were ready to do without a church, and ordained ministers, and an order of service. For men and women have very different needs.

It was when Loe told him, without any bitterness, of the persecutions suffered by all Dissenters, and by the Quakers more than any, that William's heart burned. Why—*why* should these most peaceful and inoffensive people, who would never use force at all or take up arms, be hunted down as if they were dangerous rebels or common criminals? It must be because they were not understood, had no one to speak for them in high places. Was that something that he, William Penn, friend of royalty and nobility, might be able to do? But, first, he must learn more of their way of life.

*　　*　　*

It was very quiet in the upstairs room where Friends sat, a quiet that was not empty but full of richness and the presence of God. William sat among them, feeling more and more happy and at home.

All at once there was the sound of heavy, blundering feet on the stairs, and a soldier, coarse-faced, loud-voiced, on mischief bent, stumbled into the room. He must have seen some of the plainly dressed folk assembling, and thought to have some brutal fun at their expense. William knew his type —he had had such men under his command during his military experience, and he thought he knew how to deal with it. Up he stood, a strong commanding figure, and his powerful hand gripped the fellow's collar as he propelled him toward the stair head. Another minute, and the man would have gone sprawling down the stairs.

But gentle hands were laid on William's arm. "Nay, friend William, that is not our way. No violence. If a man smite thee on one cheek, turn to him the other also."

William let go. It came to him with a shock that he was not only acting against the Friends' principles, but being very foolish as well. He had no authority over this man.

"I am sorry," he said humbly. "I might have brought trouble on you all if I had done as I wished and kicked him down stairs. Go in peace, man."

The soldier went, but not in peace. He went

straight to the magistrates and informed them that an "unlawful conventicle" was being held. In a short time he was back with a party of men and officers, who broke up the meeting and arrested nineteen of the members, William among them, and carried them before the Mayor of Cork.

The Mayor stared at William's fine clothes. "Some mistake," he said. "That's no canting Quaker! Let him go. Sir, you are at liberty."

The time had come for the final step.

"I *am* a Quaker," William announced deliberately. "I will be treated as my friends are treated. But"—here spoke the lawyer—"I require to know on what charge we are being tried."

"On the charge of being present at a tumultuous riotous assembly." Tumultuous and riotous! What a way to describe a Friends' Meeting!

"And," went on the Mayor, "unless you give bond for your good behaviour you will be committed to prison."

"And what authority," said William, "have you for such a sentence?"

"The Conventicle Act of 1662—we have had a new instruction to revive that law."

"But that law," William argued, "was passed against the Fifth Monarchy men—those who wished to overturn the State. We Friends desire no such thing—only to worship God in peace."

"What do you know of why the law was passed? Do you give bond to attend no more such meetings?"

"I do not," And so said they all. William and his companions were marched off to prison.

At the prison gates William paused, unbuckled his sword, and handed it with a bow to one of the bystanders who had gathered to gape at the spectacle of a cavalier gaoled with a bunch of Quakers.

"Henceforth," William declared, "I will walk unarmed in an armed world."

*   *   *

From prison, William wrote to his friend the Earl of Ossory, son of the Lord Lieutenant of Ireland: "Since the King's Lord Lieutenant and yourself being fully persuaded the intention of those called Quakers, by their meetings, was really the service of God, have therefore manifested a repeal by a long continuance of freedom, I hope your lordship will not now begin an unusual severity by indulging so much malice in one whose actions savour ill with his nearest neighbours [by this he meant the Mayor of Cork] but that there may be a speedy releasement to all for attending their honest calling . . ."

There was a "speedy releasement" and a stinging rebuke for the Mayor, which did not make him love the Quakers any better. William Penn had won the first round in his long battle for freedom of worship and justice.

3

FATHER AND SON

"SON William: I have writ several letters to you since I received any from you. By this I again charge you and strictly command that you come to me with all possible speed. In expectation of your compliance, I remain, Your affectionate father, W. Penn."

People had been writing to Sir William from Ireland, telling him of his son's strange behaviour —how he was attending Quaker meetings, making many friends among them, even—horrors!—that he had been imprisoned. William could see that his father was seriously upset, and no wonder; but he was still his "affectionate father" who would not condemn until he had heard what the culprit had to say for himself.

Danger and imprisonment did not daunt the young man. He even somewhat enjoyed the risk, and his new-found faith was precious, lovely— even exciting. But to wound his dear father, as he knew he must, did depress him, and it took another, sterner letter—which, however, was signed "your very affectionate father"—to convince him that he had better get it over.

One of his new friends, Josiah Coale, understood the young man's dejection, and offered to come with him to strengthen him. Coale was in his early forties, an experienced Friend who had travelled much and suffered more, and he was just the support young William needed. They arrived in London at the end of 1667. Samuel Pepys wrote in his diary with malicious glee:

". . . Mr. William Penn, who is lately come over from Ireland, is a Quaker again, or some very melancholy thing . . ."

Coale and Penn rode out to Wanstead, to the handsome new house Sir William had bought there. Sir William was awaiting them in his panelled parlour, and the first thing that shocked him was that neither his son nor his companion removed their hats when they entered.

"Give me leave, father, to present to thee my friend, Josiah Coale," began William. Sir William's eyebrows shot up, and drew down into a scowl when Coale greeted him with, "God bless thee, William Penn. I hope I see thee well?"

Sir William could not speak for a moment. In those days "thee" and "thou" was only used to servants or intimate friends. And what did the fellow mean by not giving him his title? He controlled himself, however; after all, Coale was his guest, even if uninvited; and replied courteously, if rather shortly. Coale, after commending William to his father's kindness, tactfully took his leave, and father and son faced each other alone. Then the storm broke.

"How dare you, son William! To 'thee' and

26

'thou' me—your father—as if I were a scullion!
To keep your hat on your head—where's your
respect? What of your upbringing? If your Quaker
friends are going to make you put off the manners
of a gentleman, it's worse even than I thought!"

This was a bad beginning. "Father," William
answered with all the gentleness he could muster,
"Indeed I mean no disrespect. I speak thus in
obedience to God."

"Is it obedience to God to behave like a boor?
You must have taken leave of your senses!"

"Before God," William explained, "all men are
accounted equal. That is why Josiah Coale did not
use your title. We use no titles, not even Mister or
Mistress, but only the plain name of every man or
woman."

To the bewildered Admiral this was stark non-
sense. "Do as you like among your friends," he
retorted, "but to me, and to the King and the Duke
of York, you will say 'you'—aye, and take off your
hat, too!"

"I am sorry"; William tried to speak steadily,
"but I can make no difference in my speech—no,
not to the King himself."

"At least you would remove your hat before
him!"

"These marks of respect, so-called, are but vain
shows. Honour and respect come from the heart."

Sir William's face grew purple and the veins
started out on his forehead. Could this be his beloved son, his pride and hope? Grief and anger

nearly choked him. William looked at him sorrow-fully, but without a sign of yielding. He understood perfectly what his father was feeling.

"We'll talk no more of this tonight," said Sir William abruptly. "It grows late. Go to bed, but see you are up early to drive with me in the morning."

It would have been easier if they had not loved each other so much. William watched his father drag his lame foot up the broad oak staircase, and knew that the worst was still to come. He did not sleep much that night. What did his father mean to do? Drive to Whitehall, confront William with the King or the Duke, and see if his resolution would hold?

But next morning the Admiral only ordered the coachman to drive round the countryside. Shut up together, where no one could overhear or interrupt, Sir William brought all his guns to bear on his son. He spoke of the disgrace, of the danger—danger even of death, if he should get mixed up in any of the plots that were always being hatched in that turbulent, uneasy time. No one knew better than Sir William how dangerous it was to be a noncon-formist. However innocent one might be, suspicion was always likely to fall, and the Admiral had many enemies who would rejoice, like Samuel Pepys, to see him disgraced. William replied that he, too, knew all the dangers—but he could not disobey the voice of God in his heart. Sir William pleaded—see what a splendid career was open to him if only he would see sense! Think of the good he might do! Couldn't he help his friends better from a position of power? But William had faced that, too, and made his decision. The way of the world was not for him.

So they wrangled on and on, while the coach jolted and swayed through the wintry countryside, and the coachman wondered what on earth his master meant by this aimless round and round in the bitter weather. But neither could the father move the son from his resolution, nor the son make the father understand his convictions.

They stopped at last outside an inn. "Let us," said Sir William dourly, "go in and cool our throats."

He led the way into a private room and promptly locked the door. What now? William wondered. Was he going to get a thrashing, grown man as he was? Well, better that than this endless argument. Both of them were by this time so worked up that they were almost hysterical. But Sir William, leaning on his gouty hands over the table, said in a shaking voice:

"Son William, I am going to kneel down here and pray that you may be saved from becoming a Quaker!"

At that, the sorely tried William lost control of himself. Dashing to the window he flung it open. "If thou dost," he almost shouted, "I will fling myself out!"

Luckily, at that moment came a knock at the

door, and a voice asking, "May I come in?" It was a nobleman, a friend of Sir William's, who had seen the coach at the door and thought it a good opportunity to come and have a chat. Both father and son were really glad to be saved from what was a rather ridiculous situation! They pulled themselves together, the door was opened, and in came the gentleman. Presently they were all drinking wine together, and the nobleman was congratulating Sir William on having so gifted and sensible a son. It seemed that he knew nothing about William's Quakerism, and nothing was said about it. Presently they all went off together, paid a call in the neighbourhood, and then went home without another word.

Miserable weeks followed. Though they lived in the same house, Sir William and his son hardly spoke to one another. It must have been very uncomfortable, not to say distressing, for poor Lady Penn!

*　　*　　*

William did not sit moping in idleness. He would be away for days at a time, attending Quaker meetings, and he now discovered that he had the gift of preaching. When the Spirit moved him to speak, his message was welcome, and presently he was called to speak here and there throughout the countryside. His great joy in that difficult time was to show to others the light and comfort that he had found, and bring them into a sense that God was not only their Lord and Father but their ever-present, indwelling Friend.

It was not long before he was in trouble, of course. A meeting he was attending was raided, he and other leaders were swept up and, as before, carried before the magistrate. But this magistrate knew whom he had got—the son of Admiral Sir William Penn—and he was alarmed. He was afraid to commit William to prison; instead he wrote to his father, and Sir William commanded his son to come home at once. William guessed that this latest scandal had brought matters to a head at last. Obediently he turned homeward to face whatever might be in store.

He was in Buckinghamshire at the time, and on the way home he passed through the quiet, pretty village of Amersham. In Amersham lived a notable family of Friends, the Peningtons, and William stopped at their house for a meeting, and afterwards stayed to talk.

As they sat, the door opened softly and there entered a young woman of about William's age. Her sober dress with its broad white collar and snowy cap set off a rich beauty such as William had never seen. All the fine ladies of the court were nothing to her! She had no airs and graces, no simpering smiles, but looked at him with clear eyes and steady mouth.

"Hast thou met my step-daughter?" asked Isaac Penington. "Gulielma Springett—Guli we call her. Guli, thou hast heard of William Penn?"

31

She gave him her hand and smiled, then went about her business—perhaps with just a little more colour in her cheeks because of the earnest look the young man had fixed on her. As for William, his heart was lost for good. On the way home it is very likely that he thought more of Guli Springett than of the angry father waiting for him at Wanstead.

Angry indeed Sir William was. This was the last straw. "You can pack your bags and be gone," he told William. "I've finished with you. Expect no more from me. I shall dispose of my estates to them that please me better."

William supposed he meant young brother Dick, who had never contrived to please his father much. The threat did not trouble him—he honestly set no great value on his inheritance, and luckily he had a little money of his own. As for being turned out of the house—he had seen that coming for a long time, and indeed it was best for both of them. There seemed no chance of their getting to understand one another, and perhaps time—and God— would bring them together at last. As things were, they were only irritating one another.

Sadly he hugged his weeping mother. From his father there was no parting handshake, only a last look of mingled anger and sorrow. So William Penn went forth to throw himself entirely into the life of the Friends, to share their sufferings and their faith.

4

THE BATTLE FOR JUSTICE

IN THE little room high up in the Tower of
London the July sun made the place like a
furnace; though it had been cold enough when
William Penn was locked into it in December.
That was just a year after he had parted from his
father—and what a year it had been! Sitting there
in his shirt, with the sweat rolling down his thin
face into his ragged beard—they would not let him
be visited by a barber—William had leisure to look
back and wonder whether he would ever again be
able to join in that active life among Friends. What,
after all, had he accomplished?

That visit to the King's brother, the Duke of
York, had been a failure. He had gone with his two
old friends, Thomas Loe and Josiah Coale, and
the Quaker leader George Whitehead, and the
Duke had been sympathetic—oh yes, very kind
and sympathetic to the son of his old friend. But as
for doing anything, he would not lift a finger. In
the quiet of his cell William could see why. The
Duke, a Roman Catholic, was unpopular, and he
was not going to make himself more so by taking up
the cause of the despised Quakers. After this he had
tried other powerful men at court, but still with no
result.

There was sorrow to remember. Dear Thomas Loe, his first Quaker friend, faded out of life, worn out with long travelling, hardship and persecution. But it was not altogether a sad memory.

"Bear thy Cross, stand faithful for God, and God will give thee an eternal Crown of Glory that shall not be taken from thee . . ."

"Yes," William in his cell reflected, "it is true —without the Cross we cannot win the Crown."

There followed the very unpleasant experience which finally led to his imprisonment—a quarrel with a Presbyterian minister, Thomas Vincent. This was particularly sad, for Vincent was really a very fine man who had done brave work during the terrible plague year. But like so many good men he had a blind spot. He simply could not begin to understand Friends, and in his bitterness against them he said some untrue things, "all which," Penn wrote afterwards, "we could not for the truth's sake pass in silence." One thing led to another. There was a public debate, which very nearly turned into a riot, and the Friends never got a hearing. And then William wrote his book!

He called it *The Sandy Foundation Shaken*, and in it he tried to set forth what, as a Quaker, he believed about God. But he was only twenty-four, and had not learned to express himself as clearly as he did in his later writings. At any rate, his little book was seriously misunderstood by many who read it. They thought he was denying Jesus Christ, and a howl of rage went up. This was blasphemy!

Within a month he was in the Tower, and the unlucky printer of the book as well. The authorities had caught them out on a point of law—the book had been published without a licence from the Bishop of London.

No term was set for his sentence. William was told that he must recant publicly, or remain a prisoner for the rest of his life.

"My prison shall be my grave," was his answer, "before I will budge a jot, for I owe my conscience to no mortal man. I have no fear. God will make amends for all."

But it was very hard for a young, ardent spirit like William Penn's to be shut away from everyone —from Guli Springett, whose memory was so bright in his heart. Had she been attracted to him, as he was to her? Shut away from his preaching, and from those lovely quiet meetings when the Spirit of God filled the humble room; from Friends in suffering and sorrow, whom he might have helped. The news came that good Josiah Coale was dead—and William not there to say good-bye and comfort those whom he had left.

"My soul is often heavy and bowed down in the sense of the loss of these valiants at this time of the day," he wrote in a memoir of Coale's life and work.

He heard, too, that malicious writers were putting out tracts over his signature, which cruelly misrepresented his beliefs. All this was much harder to bear than the biting cold and blistering sun, even though it robbed him of nearly all his hair! It had always been thin ever since he had had smallpox as a baby. Now he was practically bald—at twenty-four. If he ever got out of the Tower he would always have to wear a wig. Not that that would be a hardship, for most people wore wigs in those days. It would not, of course, be a great mass of curls falling almost to his waist, such as courtiers wore . . .

The sound of a key in the lock. A visitor? William looked up as the gaoler opened the door, and saw a face that had become familiar during his months of imprisonment; a youngish man in the gown of a clergyman of the Church of England—Dr. Edward Stillingfleete, Bishop of Worcester and Chaplain to King Charles II.

Charles, who still had a kindly feeling for the Penns, had sent Stillingfleete to reason with William during the early weeks of his imprisonment. "The Tower is the worst argument in the world to convince me," William had told the bishop with a grin. Stillingfleete was not offended. Indeed he took a liking to the staunch young Quaker, and came to see him more than once. They were both reasonable men. Stillingfleete took pains to understand what William had really been driving at in his *Sandy Foundation*.

"You have certainly been misunderstood," he would argue. "Now, could you not bring yourself to write another tract, explaining more clearly what you did mean? I believe that if you did this, and I presented it to the King, you could get a pardon."

At last William consented. In the quiet of his lonely room he had learned patience, and a better understanding of those who differed from him; also he had a great respect for Stillingfleete. He called his tract *Innocency With Her Open Face*, and took great pains to express himself clearly and with moderation.

Dr. Stillingfleete was smiling as he came in, and took William's hand in a warm clasp.

"The King has read your paper, and the Privy Council is considering it," he told the prisoner. "I have added my own words to it in your favour. I have every hope—indeed I am almost certain—that you will soon find yourself at liberty."

To find so good a friend in such an unexpected place was another lesson in tolerance to William Penn, and well he used it in the future.

Sure enough, it was not long before an order from the King arrived for the Lieutenant of the Tower. William Penn was to be liberated and delivered to the custody of—his father, Sir William Penn!

*   *   *

William was riding to Bristol, there to take ship for Ireland again to look over his father's estates and collect his rents. Father and son were friends once more, though they did not see eye to eye and were very careful not to get into an argument.

There was no great haste about the journey and Amersham in Buckinghamshire is not much off the direct route from Essex to Bristol, and there the Penington's would be sure to give a warm welcome to William—something of a hero since his imprisonment and his writings. And—there would be Guli. What sort of welcome would he get?

Everything went just as he had hoped. He was received as if he were already one of the family; and the look in Guli's eyes made him—almost—sure of what he wanted to know. He stayed the night with the Peningtons. It was hard to mount his horse and ride away the next day; but he had only got as far as Maidenhead when he found that his servant was missing (why, we are not told. Did he run away?) At any rate, William must turn back to the Peningtons to try to find out what had happened, and it was not so easy to tear himself away again. There was another servant to be found, and of course that took time. Altogether, William spent five happy days at Amersham, and though no engagement was announced, it was well understood between him and Guli that, when they saw the way clear, they would be married.

*   *   *

"Dined at Thomas Mitchell's. Visited the prisoners," wrote William in his diary soon after his arrival at Cork.

His own time in the Tower seemed luxury compared with what he found Friends were suffering in Ireland. Eighty men and women were packed into one small room, with no food or drink except what sympathizers could push in through a hole—and servants who had tried to bring them comforts were set in the stocks. Even children were suffering this cruel punishment—for what? Merely for attending their peaceful meetings, which were called "riotous assemblies".

His father's affairs would have to wait. William dashed off a couple of letters to the stewards, and promptly went to interview the Mayor of Cork, his old enemy. That self-important Quaker-hater merely sneered, and William saw that nothing would be gained by arguing with *him*. He must try what he could do at headquarters, so off he went to Dublin, accompanied by some Quaker leaders who had somehow escaped imprisonment.

The Mayor of Dublin, who bore the magnificent name of Desmynières, was a pompous person with an explosive temper. The gentle reasonableness of the Quakers' plea for justice only made him despise them.

"Rogues, rascals, whelps!" he shouted at them. "You ought to be whipped out of town and sent to work on the plantations!" And seizing their petition he ripped it up and flung it on the ground. William shut his lips tightly—he had a temper too—and the deputation retired without a word more.

If the Mayor thought he was done with William Penn, he was much mistaken. The Penns still had friends in high places. Beginning with government officials, he went higher and higher, and wrote at last to his acquaintances in the nobility. The Earl of Drogheda received him civilly, and invited him to dinner to meet the Earls of Arran and Roscommon, old friends of his father. If they were amused at the Quaker who carried himself with the grace of a cavalier, yet wore no sword and would not bow or sweep off his hat, and who addressed them as "thee" and "thou" in the cultivated voice of a patrician, they did not show it. They were friendly and listened to all he had to say. William began to have some hopes. He and the leading Friends drew up a carefully worded petition, setting out the grievances of the prisoners, and presented it to the Lord Lieutenant of Ireland.

Bitter disappointment! Going eagerly to the Council meeting where the petition was to be discussed, he found that it was not even mentioned. Then the Lord Lieutenant fell ill—and that seemed the end of that.

Not for William Penn. If the Council as a whole would not listen, he would tackle every official separately, over and over again, repeating the tale of the unjust suffering of innocent men, women and children until the facts stuck in their brains and could not be got rid of. Patience, persistence, gentleness, reasonableness won at last. On November 29, little more than a month after he had landed in Ireland, he was able to set down in his diary:

"Friends were released in this city (Dublin) with great love and civility from the judges."

But the Friends in Cork were still imprisoned, and no orders had been sent for their release. There was another long struggle for William Penn, and he had his father's affairs to attend to as well. There was trouble among some of the tenants that had to be settled. The discouraging months went by—January, February, March, April, May. . .

William Penn gave a dinner party for some of the noblemen of his acquaintance. They came in their coats of silk, satin or velvet, embroidered waistcoats reaching to their knees, silk stockings, diamond buckled shoes. Their host received them in his plain coat, his linen unfrilled but snowy clean. The dinner was good, and he entertained them with such charm and graciousness that they were quite enchanted. Hearing that there was to be a Quaker Meeting the next day, Sunday—First Day according to Friends' way of speech—several of them attended it to hear William Penn speak!

On the Monday the hard nut was cracked at last. Penn saw the Lord Lieutenant and obtained his firm promise that the prisoners should be released. On the same day he wrote in his diary:

"My father's business is also done." Now he could go home.

5

THE RIGHTS OF ENGLISHMEN

THE door of the meeting house in Gracechurch Street, London, was barred and soldiers stood on guard outside, but Friends had assembled as usual for their First Day meeting. They could not get in, so they stood patiently outside. The Word of God could reach them as well there as within the familiar room. This was no new thing to them. Three months before, George Fox had come to address them, been arrested and taken before the Lord Mayor. Fox maintained that the Conventicle Act did not apply to Friends, who were a peaceable people who never plotted an insurrection. The Lord Mayor let him go with a warning, but the meeting house remained closed. A month later George Whitehead tried again—he was arrested and fined. Now came William Penn, fresh from his success in Ireland, and determined to put matters to the test.

His was a great name now, not only as the son of Admiral Sir William Penn, but in his own right as a champion of justice. When it became known that he was to be present at the meeting, in the open air at the corner of Gracechurch Street and Lombard Street, the crowd was swelled by a multitude of onlookers, some merely curious, some sympathetic, some mocking. Strongly the Spirit moved in him, and quietly but fearlessly he stood forth and preached the Word of God.

News of his coming had, of course, reached the authorities, and it was not long before he and another leader of the Friends, William Mead, were seized by the constables. There was no need for violence. The two went peaceably enough. Where were they being taken? Would it be Newgate, that notorious prison where they would be thrust in among common felons, thieves, murderers, highway robbers? No, it was not to be quite so bad as that, though bad enough. They were shut up in a tavern called the "Black Dog", which was used as a kind of Annexe to Newgate for special prisoners. William Penn was certainly a special case.

That was on August 14, 1670. On September 1 they were brought to the Old Bailey to stand trial, for they had refused to pay fines on the ground that they were illegally arrested, and demanded to be tried by a jury. There presiding sat the Lord Mayor, Sir Samuel Starling, attended by the Recorder, five aldermen, three sheriffs, the constables and the clerks of the court. Penn and Mead saw no sign of mercy in their faces—only a malicious satisfaction. They had caught a fine bird in William Penn, and they meant to pluck him! Penn turned his eyes to the jury, twelve good citizens, honest plain gentlemen not very well up in the law, but wishful to do their duty if somebody would make it clear to them what it was. In them lay not only the immediate hope of the prisoners, but, if they could be made to see it, the hope of justice in England in the years to come. Penn and Mead, both of them acquainted with the law, would show them their duty if it could be done!

"That William Penn, gentleman, and William Mead, linendraper, with divers other persons . . . in the street called Gracechurch Street, unlawfully and tumultuously did assemble and congregate themselves together, to the disturbance of the peace of the said Lord the King. And the aforesaid William Penn by agreement between him and William Mead . . . then and there in the open street, did take upon himself to preach and speak . . . by reason whereof a great concourse and tumult of people in the street aforesaid, then and there, a long time did remain and continue, in contempt of the said Lord King, and of his law; to the great disturbance of his peace, to the great terror and disturbance of his liege people and subjects, to the ill example of all others in the like case offenders . . ."

The indictment made it sound very bad. But surely the jury must know enough about Quakers by this time to be sure they would never be guilty of raising a tumult or inspiring terror? Only would they have the courage to speak their minds?

"What say you, William Penn and William Mead, are you guilty, as you stand indicted, or not guilty?"

"It is impossible," retorted Penn, "that we

should be able to remember the indictment verbatim, and therefore we desire a copy of it, as is usual."

Before they could have a copy, said the Recorder, they must first plead guilty or not guilty.

"Then I ask two things," said Penn, speaking for them both. "First, that no advantage shall be taken of me if I plead without seeing the indictment; and second, that you will promise me a fair hearing, and liberty of making my defence."

"No advantage shall be taken of you. You shall have liberty, you shall be heard."

"Then I plead not guilty." And so also said William Mead.

That was the end of the morning's session, and the prisoners were marched back to the "Black Dog". Next morning's trial began with a silly squabble, designed to make them look foolish. Both of them had somehow lost their hats.

"Sirrah," demanded the Lord Mayor of the constable, "who bade you put off their hats? Put on their hats again."

Hats were crammed on to their heads. Now for the fun.

"Do you know where you are?" said the Recorder with pretended indignation.

Penn knew what was coming. "I do," he answered. "This is a court, I suppose the King's court."

"Do you know that there is respect due to the court?"

"Yes."

"Why do you not pay it then?"

"I do so."

"Why do you not put off your hat then?"

"Because I do not believe that to be any respect."

"Well, the court fines you forty marks apiece, for contempt of court."

Penn turned the tables then. "I desire," he said, with a twinkle, "that it may be observed that we came into court with our hats off, and if they have been put on since, it was by order of the bench, and not from us; and therefore not we, but the bench, should be fined."

Laughter in court. One to the Quakers!

Now the witnesses were called, but though they were ready enough to swear that they had *seen* Penn speaking, none of them could say that they heard what he was saying. Penn was quick to point out that one of them at least contradicted himself. More laughter in court, and some cat-calls. The last thing the prisoners wanted was a real "tumult".

"I desire," said Penn, "that we may come more close to the point, and that silence be commanded in the court."

In the hush that followed the beadle's "Oyez! Silence in court, on pain of imprisonment", Penn began his statement.

"We confess ourselves to be so far from recanting, or declining to vindicate the assembling of ourselves to preach, pray, or worship the eternal, holy, just God, that we declare to all the world that

46

we do believe it to be our indispensable duty . . .
nor shall all the powers on earth be able to divert
us from reverencing and adoring our God, Who
made us."

"You are not here for worshipping God," interrupted one of the sheriffs, "but for breaking the
law."

"We have broken no law. On what law are we
being prosecuted?"

"On the Common Law," said the Recorder.

"Where is this Common Law?"

"Do you think I can go over so many years, and
so many cases, which we call Common Law, just
to satisfy your curiosity?" sneered the Recorder.

"If it be so common," commented Penn, "it
should not be so hard to produce."

"*Will* you plead to your indictment?" exclaimed
the exasperated Recorder.

"How can I?" Penn returned. "How can the jury
give a verdict unless they know what law I am supposed to have broken?"

"You are a saucy fellow. Speak to the indictment."

Then Penn made that great statement which is
now a commonplace in our English courts of law;
but in those days, when juries were used to being
browbeaten by the judge, sounded bold indeed.

"I say, it is my place to speak to matter of law.
I am arraigned a prisoner; my liberty, which is next
to life itself, is now concerned; you are many
mouths and ears against me, and if I must not be

allowed to make the best of my case, it is hard; I say again, unless you show me, and the people, the law you ground your indictment upon I shall take it for granted your proceedings are merely arbitrary."

"You are troublesome. Plead to your indictment," insisted the Recorder.

"I have only asked one question so far—this question of the Common Law under which you say I am accused."

"You can ask questions till tomorrow morning, and be none the wiser!"

"I must plainly tell you——" Penn was deadly serious, and both jury and audience strained to catch every word—"that if you will deny me that hearing of the law, which you say I have broken, you do at once deny me an acknowledged right, and evidence to the whole world your resolution to sacrifice the privileges of Englishmen to your sinister and arbitrary designs."

"Take him away!" shouted the Recorder.

"Take him away!" cried the Mayor. "Shut him up in the bale-dock!" This was a sort of cage in a corner of the court-room, used to shut up obstreperous prisoners.

"I am not to be silenced," cried Penn as they pushed him in, "in a case where I am so much concerned, and not only myself, but so many ten thousand families beside!"

Now it was Mead's turn. The point he made, turning to the jury and speaking with calm impressiveness, was this: "If the Recorder will not tell you what makes a riot, a rout, or an unlawful assembly, Coke, he that was once Lord Coke (Chief Justice in the reign of James I) tells us what makes a riot, a rout, and an unlawful assembly. A riot is when three or more are met together to beat a man, or to enter forcibly into another man's land, to cut down his grass, his wood, or break down his pales."

"I thank you," said the Recorder, sweeping off his hat with a mocking bow, "for explaining to me the law."

"Thou mayest put on thy hat," replied Mead sarcastically. "I have never a fee for thee now."

After some more futile argument, Mead too was dragged away from the dock. The Recorder turned to the jury and bade them, *at their peril*, observe that witnesses had testified to seeing both Penn and Mead at an unlawful and tumultuous assembly: which was as good as ordering them to return a verdict of guilty.

"I appeal to the jury," shouted Penn through the bars of his cage, "who are my judges, and to this great assembly, whether the proceedings of this court are not most arbitrary, and void of all law, in offering to give the jury their charge in the absence of the prisoners . . ." he would have added "from the dock" but the Recorder interrupted.

"Why you *are* present," he said mockingly. "You do hear, do you not?"

Penn's naturally fiery temper boiled up. Gripping

the bars with his strong hands, he hoisted himself up and shouted over them, "No thanks to the court, that command me into the bale-dock; and you of the jury take notice, that I have *not* been heard, neither can you legally depart the court, before I have been fully heard, having at least ten or twelve material points to offer in order to invalidate their indictment—"

"Pull that fellow down!" ordered the Recorder furiously.

Mead now called out, "Are these according to the rights and privileges of Englishmen, that we should not be heard, and the jury to have their charge given them in our absence? I say these are barbarous and unjust proceedings!"

Nevertheless they were hustled away and locked up in a stifling room, while the jury were ordered to consider their verdict. But the prisoners' bold words had done their work. Although eight of the jury were inclined to be cowed by the threats of the Mayor and Recorder, four stood out firmly that the proceedings were illegal.

An hour and a half passed, the court was impatient, the spectators restless and noisy. The jury were sent for, and announced that they could not agree. The Recorder at once spotted the leader of the opposition, Edward Bushel.

"Sir, you are the cause of this disturbance," he said menacingly. "I shall set a mark on you, sir!"

One of the sheriffs added, "I know you, Mr. Bushel! You deserve to be indicted more than any man that hath been brought to the bar this day."

The jury were sent back to try again. Undaunted, Bushel and his three supporters stuck to their point. At last the whole twelve returned, and announced that they had reached agreement.

Excitement and triumph in the court! The Mayor took his seat again, the Recorder and sheriffs took their places, the prisoners were fetched in, the crowd was all agog to hear the verdict. No one doubted what it would be.

"Look upon the prisoners at the bar. How say you? Is William Penn guilty of the matter whereof he stands indicted, or not guilty?"

There was a breathless hush, into which the answer of the foreman of the jury dropped, word by word.

"Guilty—of speaking in Gracechurch Street."

Amazed at such impudence, scarlet with rage, the Mayor could scarcely believe his ears.

"Wasn't it an unlawful assembly? You mean he was speaking to a tumult of people there?"

"My lord," returned the foreman stubbornly, "that was all I was commissioned to say."

"You shall be locked up until you have given a verdict!" thundered the Mayor, and the Recorder and sheriffs added their threats of what would happen to them.

"We *have* given a verdict," said the foreman.

"Then go and consider it again!"

Back they came in half an hour, and presented

51

the Clerk with a piece of paper. "Here is our verdict," he said.

The Clerk read aloud; "We, the jurors hereafter named, do find William Penn to be guilty of speaking or preaching to an assembly, met together in Gracechurch Street, the fourteenth of August last, 1670; and that William Mead is not guilty of the said indictment."

"You shall not be dismissed until we have a verdict the court can accept," stormed the Recorder. "You shall be locked up without meat, drink, fire or tobacco. We will have a verdict by the help of God, or you shall starve for it!"

Thereupon Penn shouted indignantly that the jury ought not to be threatened, that their verdict should be free, and he warned the jury that if they yielded they would be forfeiting their rights as Englishmen.

To their everlasting honour the twelve stood firm, though they were locked up all that night and the next night too. Haggard and pale, on the fourth morning they staggered into court, and the foreman asked that the written verdict be given back to them. Broad smiles on the faces of the court.

"That paper was no verdict," said the Mayor graciously. "You shall not suffer for it."

Again the Clerk asked in form, "Is William Penn guilty or not guilty?"

"NOT GUILTY!"

"Then," said William Penn, "since we are acquitted, we may go free?"

With infinite malice the Mayor replied, "Oh no. You are committed to Newgate for your fines."

"Fines? What fines?"

"For contempt of court—you and your precious jury too!"

So to filthy, stinking Newgate they went, all fourteen of them. Power was in the hands of the Mayor and his court, but victory was to the Quakers and the noble four. The case made such a stir that, after a year of wrangling in the courts the justices of England pronounced that a jury could not be punished for its verdict, and that the jury had been illegally fined and imprisoned. William Penn had struck a great blow for justice and the rights of Englishmen.

*　　*　　*

"Dear Father," wrote William from Newgate, "I desire thee not to be troubled at my present confinement. I could scarcely suffer on a better account, nor by a worse hand, and the will of God be done. It is more grievous and uneasy to me that thou shouldst be so heavily exercised, God Almighty knows, than any living worldly concernment. I entreat thee not to purchase my liberty."

But Sir William was dying, and he longed for his elder son, now dearer to him than ever before. He paid the fines for William and for Mead, and so the champion came home—just in time.

Between the two there was now perfect love and

confidence. The sick man leaned on his strong son, and turned his thoughts to God. He thought also of his son's future, and almost with his last strength wrote to the King and the Duke of York, commending William to their friendship. He received a kindly answer from them both, and it may be that this last letter helped to bring about the crowning work of William's life.

"Son," whispered the Admiral as William bent over his bed, "Be not troubled at disappointments ... if they may be recovered, do it ... if they can't, trouble is in vain." Wise words! It almost seems as if Sir William had a glimpse of the future.

Then he sank into delirium, and then into unconsciousness, and on September 16, 1670, he died.

6

GULI

"Your jails and prisons we defy,
By bonds we'll keep our liberty,
Nor shall your racks or torments make
Us, e'er our meetings to forsake—"

NOT very good poetry, and strange lines to be
sent in a love-letter! But Guli Springett must
have smiled over them while her heart ached, for
they were written from Newgate after all. After his
father's death Penn, now a rich man, for he had
inherited all Sir William's estates, threw himself
more heartily than ever into his preaching and en-
couraging Friends. Of course he was soon arrested.
and convicted under the Five Mile Act. This Act
forbade any nonconformist minister to come within
five miles of any town where they had ever
preached. As Penn pointed out, the Act did not
apply to him, since he was not an ordained minister.
But they gave him six months in Newgate all the
same.

"Only six months?" Penn asked in surprise.
"Thou knowest a longer imprisonment would not
have daunted me."

They may have been thankful they did not give
a longer sentence, for from his prison Penn poured

out tract after tract—in defence of liberty of conscience, on Friends' beliefs and way of life, on the rights of the law, and these writings were printed and made their way all over the country. What was in the letters that went to Guli at Amersham we do not know, except for that one scrap of verse. But as soon as he was again at liberty he rode for Buckinghamshire with a lover's speed.

Guli knew that if she married Penn she would never have a peaceful home life. Always he would "seek first the Kingdom of God", and their own happiness would have to come second. Maybe she had hoped for a speedy wedding, but when Penn told her of a duty which called him away, she agreed without a protest. After all, they were perfectly sure of one another.

There were groups of Friends by this time here and there on the Continent, especially in Holland and Germany, and Penn, with two companions, was commissioned to visit and encourage them. He was away from England for three months in 1671, and when he returned he found Friends in Suffolk suffering under a particularly malicious persecution. Of course he had to stay to help them with his influence and legal knowledge. Guli waited.

At last, on April 4, 1672, in a little house at Chorley Wood in Buckinghamshire, Gulielma Springett and William Penn sat side by side, facing a party of Friends who had gathered to witness their marriage. It was as sober a wedding party as ever was seen. No white gown, no ornaments for

the bride, no bright silks and velvets for the guests.
All the colours were grave greys and browns, set
off by the snowy collars and caps of the women and
the neat neckbands of the men. But lovely Guli's
sweet face needed no finery, and the strong face
and robust body of the bridegroom would have
made him a notable figure in any company.

The little, low-ceilinged room was very still. It
grew quieter and quieter as waves of love and
prayer went out to the two young people. At last
the right moment came. William and Guli looked
at one another. They stood up, clasped hands, and
in plain simple words they took one another for
man and wife, promising to be loving and faithful
all their lives. They sat down again, and one after
another the Friends rose and gave their blessing,
advice and cheer. Finally the marriage contract was
signed and witnessed. The four years of waiting
were over. William and Guli were man and wife.

7

PENNSYLVANIA

WOULD it never end, the harassing, the fines, imprisonment, stocks? Were Friends never to know peace and an ordered life, they whose whole faith was based on love, peace and goodwill? It had gone on for so long, for even during the Protectorate Quakers had been mobbed and harried. There were youngsters on the verge of manhood and womanhood who had never known security. It was very difficult to keep from bitterness under so much injustice!

George Fox, their leader, was arrested on the usual charge of holding an unlawful meeting; but, he would not take the oath before the court. Friends hold literally to Christ's command, "Swear not at all", and say that one must speak truth at all times, so Fox was kept in prison, and an old law was brought up which would have kept him in there for ever. William Penn led a group who fought in the law courts for more than a year against this twisting of the law, and won at last; but all over the country meetings were being broken up, Friends bled white by fines, and worn down by continued persecution. They stood firm and kept the faith—but surely it was not for this that they lived?

Penn and Guli had sorrows of their own to bear. Their first three babies only lived for a few weeks, and William's young brother, Dick, died at the age of eighteen. But in 1675 a boy was born whom they named Springett, after Guli's parents, and he lived to grow up. Then came a daughter, Letitia, lovingly called Tishe, and finally another boy, William, always known as Bille.

Thoughts began to turn westward. Across the wide Atlantic Ocean, on the shores of the still new continent of America, colonies were growing up. In the reign of the King's grandfather, James I, the Pilgrim Fathers had fled from persecution to settle in the north. In the south, great tracts of land, whole countries which were to become States, had been granted to nobles such as Lord Baltimore and Lord Delaware. In those almost untouched lands, would there be a refuge for Friends, where they could build up their way of life unmolested, and show the world that, given a chance, the Way of Peace would work?

George Fox and other Quakers had visited America. They reported that, sad to say, the Puritans who had settled in New England would not grant to others the freedom of worship they claimed for themselves. Even there little groups of Friends were persecuted and driven out. Then came a wonderful gleam of hope.

Westward from New York the mighty river Delaware winds its way from north to south to open in to the splendid Delaware Bay. Between the river and the coast, south of New York, lies what is now the State of New Jersey; and the western part of New Jersey, along the bank of the Delaware, came into the hands of a group of Quaker trustees, of whom Penn was one. The story is too complicated to go into here! But here at last was a place where Friends might safely settle, and from 1675 onward parties of Friends set out, prepared to conquer the wilderness and make happy homes where their children might grow up in freedom.

But the problem was not yet solved. West New Jersey could not hold all those who wished to emigrate.

*   *   *

England, Penn saw, was ruled by selfish, greedy, corrupt men. The only chance for reform was to get some honest men into Parliament. None of the Friends could stand, because they could not take the Oath which every Member of Parliament had to take; but there were other men, anxious for reform, whose consciences did not forbid them to take the oath. Would it not be right to join with them in working for a better state of affairs? Penn decided that it would.

Not far from his home at Warminghurst in Sussex lay the estate of Penshurst, and there lived Algernon Sidney, who had been a friend of Cromwell (he was a great-nephew of the famous Philip Sidney of the reign of Queen Elizabeth the First). Algernon Sidney was a Whig—that is, of the new party which opposed the Tory party in power. Sidney was the kind of upright man whom Penn wished to see in Parliament, and he persuaded him to stand. Sidney was defeated, but William Penn had become famous as a Whig, and the Court party, who had always hated him for his speaking and writing against injustice, were out for his blood. If he could be proved a rebel and traitor— and many of the pamphlets he had written could be twisted to sound as if he wished to overthrow the State—his life would be forfeit.

Did poor Guli, with three little children to care for, ever wish her husband were less brilliant, less brave? She must have suffered agonies of anxiety, but we have no hint that she ever murmured.

Then came that sudden, astonishing twist to affairs that saved Penn, that gave the Friends a refuge and a great opportunity, and influenced the history of America.

Whose idea was it—William Penn's—or the King's—or the Duke of York's? We shall never be sure.

Admiral Penn, as we have seen, was a devoted friend of the Stuarts. When Charles II was in exile Penn had "lent" him a considerable sum of money, about £11,000, which was a great deal in those days. But many others had "lent" great sums to the Stuarts, and Charles certainly never troubled himself about repaying those debts!

The Duke of York held a grant of land in America, a huge, almost untouched wilderness west of the Delaware river. He could give it to whom he pleased. But what a howl of fury would go up from the Tories if he granted it to a "parcel of rascally Whigs!"

But, shrewd Charles perceived, what an excellent way of getting rid of a multitude of these same Whigs who called themselves Friends and whom others called Quakers!

And—both the King and the Duke of York respected Penn, and would be glad to get him out of the way of peril.

Very well then. Let the published reason be that the Duke of York granted the land west of the Delaware River, south of New York and north of Maryland, to William Penn in repayment of the debt owed to his father.

"The government at home was glad to be rid of us at so cheap a rate as a little parchment to be practised in a desert 3,000 miles off," wrote Penn, who understood perfectly.

William Penn became the absolute proprietor, subject only to the King, of a country nearly as big as England; to make and publish laws with the assent of the people, to establish judges and other officers, to pardon and abolish crimes (except treason and murder)—in fact, to be almost a prince. The whole affair went through extraordinarily quickly. On March 5, 1681, Penn wrote to his friend Robert Turner:

. . . "This day my country was confirmed to me under the Great Seal of England, with large powers and privileges, by the name of Pennsylvania; a name the King would give it in honour of my father . . .I feared lest it should be looked on as a vanity in me, and not as a respect in the King, as it truly was, to my father, whom he often mentions with praise. Thou mayest communicate my grant to Friends, and expect shortly my proposals.

It is a clear and just thing, and my God that has given it me through many difficulties will, I believe, bless and make it the seed of a nation."

*　　*　　*

Several ship-loads of Friends sailed for Pennsylvania before the Proprietor was able to follow them. There was so much to do—the "Frame of Government", or general laws for the province, to draw up and submit to leading Friends; the selection of the pioneers, who must be of good character, healthy and not afraid of hard work; his own affairs to set in order; Penn had a thousand things to think of at once, and though he had many able and willing helpers, the responsibility for everything rested finally upon his shoulders. And in the midst of it all he somehow found time to write his finest piece of work that beautiful little book called *No Cross, No Crown*. Christians of many denominations today still read it, and find strength and courage.

His care, too, was not only for the European settlers in the new province. His subjects there would be also the first dwellers, the Red Indians, men with their own rights as human beings. One of his first concerns was to reassure them that they would not be ruthlessly dispossessed, as too often had happened in other settlements. In September, 1681 he wrote them a long and tender letter telling them that he would treat them as brothers in God and see that they had justice.

That these were not empty words he was to prove in time.

*　　*　　*

"Now that I am to leave thee, and that without knowing whether I shall ever see thee more in this world, take my counsel into thy bosom, and let it dwell with thee in my stead while thou livest," wrote Penn in a long letter of advice and instruction to Guli.

The time of his sailing was drawing very near. The Atlantic was wide and ships were small and dependent on wind and current. So many things might happen before they could meet again, for Guli could not come with him. She was expecting another child.

To Springett, aged seven: "My dear Springett, be good, learn to fear God, avoid evil, love thy book, be kind to thy brother and sister and God will bless thee and I will exceedingly love thee. Farewell, dear child. Thy dear father, Wm. Penn."

To Letitia, aged five: "Dear Letitia, I dearly love thee and would have thee sober [that is, steady and sensible]; learn thy book, and love thy brothers.

I will send thee a pretty book to learn in. The Lord bless thee and make a good woman of thee. Farewell . . ."

And to little William, aged two: "Dear Bille, I love thee much, therefore be sober and quiet, and learn his book. I will send him one, so the Lord bless thee. Amen."

Three precious little letters, enclosed in Guli's letter, to be read over and over to the children while their father was away.

8

THE GREAT ADVENTURE

APPLES were reddening on the orchard boughs when the ship *Welcome* glided into Delaware Bay in October 1682. The passengers—what were left of them—haggard, unkempt and staggering with weakness, crowded to the rails to refresh their eyes with the sight of green lawns where the deer came down to drink, trim farmsteads, and behind and between them the primeval forest, dense and a little threatening. This was West New Jersey, wild enough still, and beyond it, up the river, the still wilder land they were come to make their own. Some of them were a little daunted, and turned to gain courage from the cheery, confident smile of their leader.

It had been a dreadful voyage. Though the weather had been kind enough, smallpox had broken out on board, and in the crowded, uncomfortable quarters there was no way of stopping it from spreading. Thirty-one passengers died—and in the midst of the fear and misery a baby was born. Penn had cause to be thankful that the disease had struck him as a baby, even though it cost him his hair. It meant he could not catch it a second time. He might not greatly value his own life, but it would have been disaster for his province if he had died at sea. Looking after the sick, comforting the dying and reassuring the frightened, he became not so much the leader as the elder brother of all on board.

The first pause was made at New Castle, New Jersey. This was the first sizeable settlement the travellers had seen, and it looked comfortingly English. A tall windmill made a striking landmark, the meadows where plump contented cattle grazed were preserved from flooding by dykes such as one sees in East Anglia. In fact they had been made by the Dutch settlers who founded the little town. But a big fort of solid logs spoke of the dangers of frontier life, and the buildings round about were all of wood, strongly built, but plain and rough to eyes fresh from old England. Not that they minded that.

News of their coming had gone before them, and the water-front was crowded with as mixed an assembly as one could imagine. Here were Swedes and Dutch and English, and among them the bare brown shoulders and befeathered top-knots of red Indians—shy and curious, wondering just what the coming of the new Great Chief would mean to them.

There in the forefront was a familiar face— William Markham, whom Penn had sent out as his representative with the first ship-load of Adventurers. With him was a number of leading citizens, all welcoming and very respectful. It was a great moment for Penn when for the first time he put his foot on the soil of America, and was presented with the key of the fort and a piece of turf with a tiny tree planted in it—token that the inhabitants of New Castle peacefully yielded him the town and the lands surrounding it.

But this was not the end of the voyage. Further up the Delaware lay the village of Upland now called Chester, nearer to the site chosen for Philadelphia, which was to be the capital of Pennsylvania. There the Adventurers disembarked at last, and found a hearty welcome in the homes of Friends who had already settled there. After the dirt and discomfort, smells and sickness of the ship, what a relief to wash thoroughly without the basin upsetting, to put on fresh clothes and eat good wholesome food from the crops gathered on this fertile soil! But greater than any of these homely blessings was the sense of freedom, peace and hope in a land that was their own!

Not that there was much peace for William Penn. Though Markham and his fellow commissioners had done wonders in getting affairs started, there was so much that could only be done by the Proprietor himself; and the first thing Penn did was to send out messages to say that the first Court —or Parliament—of Pennsylvania would be held in three days' time at New Castle, when the "Frame of Government" would be presented, questions of land settlement would be arranged, and, above all, government officials elected. Meanwhile—Philadelphia.

Penn had chosen the name himself, using two Greek words, *philia*, love, and *adelphos*, brother; as one might put it, the "City of Brotherly Love". That is what he hoped it would be. He had seen enough of the narrow, dark streets of London with its close-packed houses and ever-present danger of plague and fire to resolve that Philadelphia should not be like that. "Be sure to make your choice where it (the river) is most navigable, high, dry and healthy," he had written to Markham from England; and "that it be a green country town, which will never be burned, and always be wholesome." Among many other things, William Penn was one of the first planners of a Garden City. Now he took a canoe and was paddled a few miles up the Delaware to the place selected.

His heart lifted as the shores slipped by. What a country! Such woods—walnut, sycamore, cypress, chestnut, hickory, beech and oak; squirrels chattering angrily from the branches, rabbits scudding away from human voices, a crash as a great-antlered elk lifted its head from feeding among the lily-pads and thundered into the undergrowth. Up a side stream he glimpsed a beaver dam, promising fur useful for trade. The river, his companions told him, was full of fish; whales sometimes came right into Delaware Bay. It was a healthy country—people often lived to be a hundred here. (One wonders how they knew that, since the country was so newly settled. But perhaps they referred to the Indians.)

The land now rose in low cliffs on either side, broken on the west by a creek with a wide mouth and sandy beach just fit for making a haven for ships. A wharf was built already, and as Penn's boat swung round to enter the creek, canoes manned by Indians and settlers shot out to welcome and escort the Governor home. Ten houses had already been built.

"Thou hast chosen well," Penn told Markham as they paced the line of the wide main street. It ran east-west for two miles, from the Delaware to another, smaller river. In his mind's eye Penn saw it bordered by gracious, well-built houses, each in its own spacious garden, shaded by trees, with other streets crossing it in a grid pattern, and in the centre an open park.

"To turn for a little to my own matter," said Penn at last, "I would see the place thou hast chosen for my own home."

"Thou shalt see it tomorrow," Markham promised, "But it lies twenty-four miles up the river, and today it is too late. We shall rest tonight at the Blue Anchor Inn, where Captain Dare will be proud to receive thee."

The "Blue Anchor" was really old, ten years at least, put up as a trading post before ever Pennsylvania was thought of, and Captain Dare was innkeeper, postmaster, factor and master of the ferry service—a very important inhabitant.

Penn and Markham talked over the settlement made with the Indians for the lands. "I hope they were satisfied," Penn said a little anxiously.

"They drove a good bargain and I think we have satisfied them," answered Markham. "This is what we have paid them:" He pulled a paper from his wallet and read aloud: "350 fathoms of wampum—that, thou knowest, is the strings of cowrie shells they use as money—300 Dutch guilders (they are accustomed to Dutch coins); 20 white blankets; 60 fathoms of woollen cloth; 20 guns—"

"It's to be hoped they use the guns for shooting game and not against each other," interrupted Penn grimly.

"Twenty coats," Markham continued, "forty shirts, forty pairs of stockings—"

"Do they already wish to dress like Europeans?" wondered Penn.

"Hoes, knives, glasses, pipes, scissors, combs, tobacco, rum—"

"Wait!" Penn interrupted. "I do not like that rum. The Indians are not used to strong liquor, and it will drive them mad."

"It is the usual custom to include rum in the payments."

"It shall never again be made in any payment here," said Penn firmly, and while he ruled it never was. Pity that the other states of America had not made the same decision!

Next day, as Penn paced the land, already partly cleared, where Pennsbury Manor would be built, his active mind saw it all as it would be—a home for Guli and the children, a warm and welcoming house where friends from far and near would be hospitably entertained. He pictured a flight of wide stone steps rising up from the river, where boats coming from Philadelphia could be moored; a shady avenue of trees, and at the end of it a mellow, red brick house, three stories high, with a large hall and dining-room for entertaining, smaller parlours for private talk, stables, bakehouse, laundry, still-room; a flower garden for Guli, a herb garden, orchards of apple, peach, plum, cherry. The furnishings would be simple, but of the best material and workmanship; solid oaken floors, fine panelling, delicate silver and china, books, pictures —"My children must not grow up savages, though they live in a wilderness," he reflected. The cavalier in him—the best type of cavalier, generous and hospitable—was uppermost as he planned his stately, friendly house.

But Guli never saw that lovely home.

9

THE "FRAME OF GOVERNMENT"

"GOVERNMENT seems to me to be a part of religion itself," Penn had written while still in England . . . "any government is free to the people under it where the laws rule, and the people are a party to those laws." Thinking it over he added, "But when all is said there is hardly one frame of government in the world so ill designed by its first founders that, in good hands, would not do well enough; and story tells us that the best, in ill ones, can do nothing great or good."

The rules he laid before the first Assembly for their acceptance sound very ordinary to us—free elections, no taxes except those made by law, trial by jury, all courts to be open, so that no one could be condemned in private and without a hearing; but for those days they were very modern, almost revolutionary. Free elections—in England members of Parliament so often bribed themselves into a seat that few men thought it very wrong. No taxes without the consent of law—in England taxes were often clapped on at the will of a small group; and we have already seen how trial by jury could be perverted by a bullying judge.

There was to be freedom of religion. Anyone holding office must be a Christian, but he need not be a Quaker, and no one was to be persecuted for holding any religion or none, provided he was peaceable.

There was to be no death penalty except for treason and murder (Penn would have liked to abolish it for these too, but that by his charter he could not do). In England at that time a man could be hanged for stealing anything above the value of a shilling, besides a whole list of offences now punishable by fines or imprisonment.

There were to be none of the cruel sports of bull and bear baiting or cockfighting, and no duelling. Penn remembered the silly young coxcomb in Paris who wanted to fight about the raising of a hat!

No taking of oaths in a law-court or on assuming office. "Let your yea be yea and your nay, nay," said Jesus, and the Friends obeyed it literally—as many other Christians do today.

But what really startled the Assembly was that this Governor to whom the King had given almost absolute power, proceeded to make it over to the people, and to make sure, as far as he could, that no man would ever play the tyrant over Pennsylvania, "that the will of one man may not hinder the good of a whole country." The Council itself was to frame laws and elect officials, and, if a majority so wished, amend the constitution itself. And, Penn added, "My heirs and assigns have solemnly declared, granted and confirmed . . . that neither I, my heirs nor assigns, shall procure or do anything whereby the liberties in this charter contained and expressed shall be infringed or broken."

This, together with a number of regulations about the holding of land and so forth, most necessary in a new, developing country, was laid before the first Assembly of Pennsylvania; and Penn himself tactfully left them alone for four days to discuss the whole matter, so that they would not feel embarrassed by his presence. His trust was rewarded. With a few practical additions and adjustments the whole Frame of Government was unanimously accepted. The first great step had been taken.

*   *   *

Penn had responsibility for more than the settlers, for those already in the land, the tribes of Red Indians. They had been accustomed to hunt and roam over the whole territory. They also had their rights, and somehow they must be brought into friendly relations with the Europeans, the needs of both must be safeguarded. Otherwise the country could not prosper, there would be bloody wars, hatred would spring up between the races. A country founded on injustice could never flourish.

So invitations were sent out to all the chiefs of the tribes of Pennsylvania, courteously worded, each addressed according to his proper style, to meet with the Governor, in a great council to be held in the open air under the trees, north of the city of Philadelphia. What a sight it must have been!

There in a great horse-shoe they squatted, the chiefs in the inner ring, magnificent in head-dresses of dyed feathers. Bright blankets or bare brown shoulders, beaded moccasins and buckskin shirts, fringed leggings, necklaces and belts of shells, dark solemn faces and keen black eyes, and behind them the tall forest trees making a fitting wall for this open-air council chamber.

Some had seen white men before; a few had been present at the landing of the Governor, but to most he was a stranger. How would he look? Would he be magnificent in the silks and velvets brought from that strange white man's land beyond the sea which many Indians had never seen? Would he be haughty and aloof, or stern and forbidding? On the whole they were hopeful, for the news of his kindly letter had spread widely. But white men had dealt treacherously with the tribes before, and there was some restlessness among the young braves in the background. Bows and tomahawks were laid aside, of course, as this was a peace meeting; but they would easily be fetched if things went awry.

He was coming, the Governor, the White Chief, and his "braves"! A group of dark figures, in brown or grey or black, with broad hats on their heads, walked slowly up to the rising ground at the open end of the horseshoe. The powerfully built man who was their leader was as plainly dressed as the rest, and wore only a blue sash to distinguish him.

He took his stand under a tall elm (ever afterwards called the "Treaty Elm") and spoke to them, slowly and sometimes hesitating for a word, in their own language!

Penn must have put in some hard work amid all his other business, and he must have had a natural gift, to have so quickly mastered the Indian speech; but he could hardly have made a better start. What if he did stumble a little or mispronounce a word? They loved him for having taken the trouble to learn their tongue; and he, for his part, had come to understand more of the Indian way of thought.

The Great Spirit, said Penn, was the Father of all men, whatever their colour. The feathered heads bowed agreement. That was their belief, too. The Great Spirit wished all men to behave as brothers. Brothers should trust one another and treat one another fairly. The white brothers wished to share this beautiful land with the red brothers. There was room for them all, but everything ought to be discussed peacefully in council and agreed to freely. No land should be taken by the white men from the Indians unless it was paid for at an agreed price. The Indians should promise in return that they would not harm the white men or damage their crops.

Again the feathered heads bowed. They knew that the Indians had certainly not got the worst of bargains made so far with the newcomers!

And if there should be disputes, Penn continued, he asked his Indian brothers to bring their complaints to the courts of law, where they would have a fair hearing and equal justice with the whites. He admitted that white men had often treated Indians unjustly. "And," he said, "I am not that kind of man!"

Finally, he asked that his Indian brothers would enter freely into a peaceful treaty with him and the settlers, that both sides would swear to keep sacred. Would they do so?

There was a pause, then from the ranks of chiefs and warriors went up a resounding "Hough!" of agreement. That was all that was needed—no papers to be signed or hostages given, but the honourable word of honest men. Details could be settled later—indeed Penn spent many months coming to formal decisions about land purchase— but from thenceforward they were friends.

The solemn meeting broke up. Now there were games and contests of strength. The Governor, casting off his coat, offered to wrestle with any of the young braves who cared to accept his challenge; and, it is said, he beat them all! He joined in their games and visited their wigwams, squatting on the ground and eating Indian food with his fingers. But it was not so much what he did, though that gained their respect and admiration; it was the honest, kindly heart of him that they perceived. Wherever he went men wondered at the swiftness with which he entered into the heart of the Indians. Was it because he really did believe what he professed—that God was in truth the loving Father of all races and kinds of men?

10

CLOUDS

"LOVING Friends and Tenants," wrote Penn, and paused, sending up a prayer for guidance; "I salute you and wish you well. I have sent the bearer, James Atkinson, to gather my quit-rents among you, and you must not take it hard that I press you in this matter, for you know that I receive neither custom nor taxes, but maintain my table and government at my own charges, which is what no governor doth beside myself."

Those who received grants of land in the New World expected to make money out of them by taking a percentage of all taxes and customs duties. This was the accepted thing. But Penn had not taken over Pennsylvania to make a fortune. All he asked was the small regular sum from each settler, called "quit-rent", which acknowledged him as the Proprietor. He had poured vast sums into the country, lending and giving, and he was beginning to be himself pressed for money. He sighed. Money! How he hated the detestable word! But he had his family to think of.

"I expect you will all strive to answer me herein, and so engage the kindness of your friend and landlord, William Penn."

Did he truly expect that, he wondered? He knew

that his people loved him and trusted him, but they did not understand his position. They had paid for the land they held, and did not see why they should owe an extra sum, trifling though it was. Besides, though after two years Pennsylvania was flourishing, rich with all the produce of the kindly earth, money itself was very scarce. Very well, Penn would meet them as far as he could.

"Let the planters give me credit," he wrote later, "for being willing to take my quit-rents in tobacco at twopence a pound." He was growing weary of begging—he who had given so much— "separated from the greatest comforts of my life— my wife and children—for the good of all."

His wife and children. News of them took so long in coming, and when it came it was not good. Guli had been very ill—at one time they thought she was dying. The baby she had been expecting only lived three weeks. Springett, dear bright boy, was not very strong. Penn hungered either to be with them or to have them come to him; but it was beginning to be clear that this could not be for some time yet.

*　　*　　*

For there was another worry which threatened the very life of Pennsylvania.

When the boundaries had been drawn up, in England, no one knew exactly the geography of this far off country. Right from the beginning there had been disputes with Lord Baltimore, owner and governor of Maryland to the south, as to where his land ended and Penn's began. Lord Baltimore claimed that his grant extended as far north as latitude 40—and latitude 40 ran north of Philadelphia itself! Moreover, he claimed the whole of Delaware Bay and the mouth of the Delaware River, and if this were so Pennsylvania would be completely cut off from the sea. Trade, fisheries and travel would be at Lord Baltimore's mercy.

On the other hand, Penn had it set down in his charter that his grant ran twelve miles south of the town of New Castle—and if that were so he was entitled to claim the northern strip of Maryland. It was a proper muddle, due to ignorance, but it had already provoked much ill-feeling.

True to his principles, Penn tried hard to meet Lord Baltimore and have a survey made on the spot, so that the business could be fairly settled once and for all. But Baltimore always seemed to be busy elsewhere. Settlers in the disputed territory were becoming disturbed and angry, not knowing to whom they ought to pay their taxes.

"I shall have to go to England and lay the matter before the King," Penn told his Council. "I trust I shall not be long away."

They looked grave, but agreed that it was the only thing to be done. "But thou wilt have a care of thyself," they urged him. "Keep clear of all Whig plots—remember Algernon Sidney."

There was indeed danger for Penn in England. Recently there had been a plot to murder the King and the Duke of York, a plot known as the Rye House Plot. At the same time Sidney and other Whigs had been planning to overthrow the corrupt government. Though they would certainly not have stooped so low as assassination, they were arrested as traitors, and the leaders, Sidney and Lord Russell, were executed on Tower Hill. Penn was known as a friend of Sidney. No wonder his friends on the Council were anxious.

"I will sail for England," said Penn resolutely, "as soon as I have put everything in order here."

But a year—perhaps a little more—would see him back again, he felt sure, and Guli and the children with him. Then he could settle down at lovely Pennsbury Manor, and give the rest of his life to Pennsylvania.

It was fifteen years before he returned.

*   *   *

A dying King, fretful and not in the least interested in the affairs of Pennsylvania; a heavy persecution of Quakers, and indeed all Dissenters, due to the Rye House Plot; his own affairs badly wanting attention; Guli in frail health; that was what Penn found when he arrived in England in November, 1684. It seemed he was as much needed here, apart from the dispute with Baltimore, as in America.

In February 1685 Charles II was dead and James II, formerly Duke of York, the Roman Catholic, was on the throne. That summer came the rebellion and defeat of the Duke of Monmouth—a horrible story which does not belong in these pages, except that it delayed the hearing of Penn's case and provoked a still worse oppression of Dissenters.

But Penn was still the friend of James II. In August his case was heard, and half of it settled satisfactorily; he began to have hopes.

The rest of the case dragged on. Persecution increased. Penn struggled to make James see that he was bringing disaster on himself and his country by his obstinacy; all he got was the distrust of Friends and rumours that he, Penn himself, had secretly become a Roman Catholic. And the news from Pennsylvania was bad.

Quarrels broke out between members of the Council left to govern. Penn wrote letter after letter imploring them to be at peace, as Friends should, but his presence itself was needed, and he could not come to them yet. No money came to him from quit-rents, and he was badly in debt in England.

In Holland, William of Orange, James's nephew and son-in-law, was listening to the call of the Whig Party to come over and save England from being forced into the Roman Church. But William Penn, Whig though he was, and though he disapproved of almost everything James did, remained loyal to his old friendship.

In November, 1688, William of Orange landed. James II fled.

Penn had faithfully kept out of Whig plots— and the result was that he was once more in danger of his life.

II

A MAN OF SORROWS

"WILL PENN! Dear Will!" George Fox clasped Penn's hand and looked earnestly into his face. "Thou hast been sorely troubled, I can see. But they have freed thee?"

Penn sat down heavily—he was certainly very tired.

"It's one thing," he said, "to be in the Tower when one is young and full of hope, and for a righteous cause. But to be accused of treason—a plot I did not even know about—in danger of my life for what I never did or dreamed of——"

"It is hard, Will, it is very hard to bear," Fox spoke sympathetically. "But thou knowest that William of Orange still sits uneasily on his throne—and he knows thou wast a friend to the former King."

"I can truly say," went on Penn, "that I do not greatly fear death for myself, even by the headsman's axe. But my wife—oh, George, my Guli is dying! Cares and fears for me have worn her out. If I died, what would happen to my children? Worse still, if I were convicted of treason, Pennsylvania would be forfeit—and who knows what Governor would be put in my place—one very likely who would not care for the people and love the Indians as I do——"

"Dear friend," Fox said gently, "thou must not take all the burden on thyself. Doth not the Lord love thy Guli and thy children? Hath not the Lord a care for the people of Pennsylvania? Hath He not cared for thee? See, thou art acquitted of treason and free."

Penn's face lighted up. "That is true, and I believe it," he answered. "Indeed, I am making my plans to return to America. I have already a scheme for another city, between the two rivers, that shall be as beautiful as Philadelphia. And I think—I hope—if I could take Guli away from England, into the healthful air of Pennsylvania— if I could bring her to Pennsbury—she might yet recover."

"I trust that it may be so." But Fox looked a little sadly at his friend. He had seen Guli, and knew how fast her strength was wasting.

Penn's face saddened again, and the lines of sorrow deepened. "But oh, George," he whispered, "what shall I find when I get there? They are breaking my heart with their quarrels—they are tearing me to pieces. Oh, I came to them in love, and I went away in love, meaning to come back to them in love. I am a man of sorrows, George, and they add to my griefs, not because they don't love me, but because they don't love one another."

"God's children are often wayward," said Fox. "Thou must not forget, Will, to look for the Divine Spirit deep in each heart."

Penn looked at the aged face, so lined, so pale, crowned now with snow-white hair. The Inner Light shone through the failing body, and he realized with a sharp pang that his old friend and teacher would not be with him long. He was so easily tired now, he who had been used to tramp mile after mile in rough weather and endure hardship with a song of praise!

"I must not tire thee with my troubles," he said, rising. "God bless thee. Thou hast done me good."

Six weeks later Fox lay on his death bed. His "dear Will Penn" was by his side.

"The seed of God reigns over all, and over death itself," he murmured, and fell asleep, to wake on the other side of the river.

"O, he is gone," wrote Penn to Fox's widow, "and has left us to the storm that is over our heads."

* * *

"Where is the man William Penn?" The officer of the law pushed through the crowd that was dispersing from the funeral of George Fox.

"What do you want with William Penn?"

"I have a warrant for his arrest! Hinder me at your peril."

"On what charge?" Penn's friends spoke mildly, but they stood firm, and the officer, not knowing where Penn was, had to stand still too. On the edge of the crowd, someone slipped quietly away.

"On a charge of plotting to overthrow their

Majesties, King William and Queen Mary, by procuring an invasion of the French. I say, where is he?"

"He is not here. He has left the ground."

It was true, of course. A Friend would not lie, even to save another. Penn had gone away quickly to be quiet and master his grief. The one who had slipped away followed him breathless to warn him.

"This time I will not be taken!" The lion in Penn was roused. "Friend, find out for me exactly what the charges are, and tell George Whitehead. He will pass it on to me."

When the accusation became known, Penn, in hiding in the house of a friend, was furious. A man named Fuller, in Ireland—no doubt hoping to get paid—had accused Penn of this plot, and he had been found guilty by the Grand Jury of Dublin without even being called to defend himself! It was clean against the law, but Penn knew that once he was taken and imprisoned he might be executed before he could bring proofs of his innocence.

It was a doubly bitter blow, because he was almost ready to sail for America, a company of Friends had gathered—and now everything must stop. Penn disappeared.

For three years no one but Springett, seventeen now and his father's right hand; Guli of course; and a few trusted Friends, knew his whereabouts as he moved from place to place. But out of those three years of loneliness and wandering came two precious treasures. He wrote a small book, *The*

Peace of Europe, which contains ideas that we are only just beginning to put into practice—such as the United Nations Organization; and *Some Fruits of Solitude*, a collection of wise and helpful thoughts that have comforted many sufferers.

At last it was over. Fuller the perjurer was unmasked. King William, urged by three lords who had known Penn for thirty years and could vouch for his innocence, issued a decree that he was not to be molested any longer. All charges against him were dismissed.

Too late for Guli. Penn hurried to the bed where she lay dying. He never wished to leave her side, but she would not let him stay away from Meetings.

"O go, my dearest! Don't hinder any good for me. I desire thee to go. I have cast my care upon the Lord. I shall see thee again."

One day she asked to see her children, and they anxiously gathered round her. Lovingly she looked at them—Springett, nearly twenty, so intelligent, so faithful—but delicate, not strong like his father. Tishe, seventeen, a little woman, sweet and capable. Bille, a schoolboy of fourteen—Oh Bille, so careless and so pleasure-loving, what will become of you?

"Be not frighted, children, I do not call you to take my leave of you, but to see you," whispered the mother. "I would have you walk in the fear of the Lord, and with His people in His holy truth."

At the end of February, 1694, alone with her husband and in his arms, Guli died.

12

A SECOND SPRING

HANNAH CALLOWHILL was thirty and still unmarried. That was strange, for she had a charming face and a gentle character, and she was the daughter of a well-to-do Quaker linen-draper in Bristol. She would have been a very good match for any of the young men she met among the group of Friends in that flourishing town.

Thirteen years earlier, when she was only seventeen, William Penn had visited Bristol. He was then at the height of his powers, the friend of kings, the new Proprietor of a province, full of his plans for an ideal colony of freedom and justice; glowing with enthusiasm, frank and sincere in his dealings, as became a Friend, but with a certain courtly grace which came from his cavalier upbringing.

Is it possible that this princely man made all the youths of Bristol seem just a trifle dull? At any rate, Hannah was still at home when William Penn, a widower, on a preaching tour of the West Country, came to speak at Bristol.

He was changed—over fifty, and by the standards of that time almost an old man. He was heavier, sadder—but when he spoke the old fire lit up his face, and suffering and disappointment had not embittered him, only drawn him closer still to God.

Hannah's sweet face stood out among the others, warm with friendliness and sympathy. Her hand trembled a little in his clasp—or did she respond to some strong feeling in his heart? He would never forget his Guli, but it was as if her tender spirit was leading him to a new comfort and a companion for the rest of his life.

The wooing of Hannah Callowhill was not easy. Not that her heart was not won at that Bristol meeting (or perhaps thirteen years before?), but she doubted. He was so much older—such a great man, so much above her! And then there were his children, two of them practically grown up. How could she be a mother to them? How would they feel about their father's second marriage?

She need not have feared. Springett and Tishe loved her at once, and rejoiced that their father had found happiness again. They wrote delightful letters; Tishe sent gifts of her own preserves. As for Bille, he accepted her. He was too much absorbed in himself to care one way or the other.

So there was another Quaker wedding. The only thing that marred the rejoicings was that Springett was so thin and coughed so much. The newly-married couple had hardly got home to Warminghurst when the boy had to take to his bed. He had never got over a heavy chill caught some weeks before, and neglected through not wishing to overshadow his father's marriage.

Hannah made herself his nurse, leaving the capable Tishe to look after the household as before.

"Don't thee do so," pleaded Springett as she waited on him. "Don't thee trouble thyself so much for such a poor creature as I am!" But of course Hannah would not listen to him, and tended him devotedly.

All in vain. Springett tried hard to get better. He insisted on getting up, and asked his father to take him for a coach drive, hoping it would do him good; but when they returned he had to be supported into the house.

"Really, father, I am exceedingly weak," he said. "Thou canst not think how weak I am."

He died in his father's arms on the tenth day of April, 1696. "In whom I lost all that any father can lose in a child," wrote Penn.

*   *   *

September, 1699. At last Penn was going back to America, with Hannah and Tishe. Bille was left behind—he had just got married!

Why the long delay? There had been his tangled business affairs to settle—as far as they could be cleared up, for he had neglected his own affairs, and had been badly cheated by a scheming steward.

The welcome the family had on landing fairly renewed Penn's youth, and quite startled Hannah and Tishe. They had dreaded what they might find, after the distressful letters exchanged through all those years. But it was clear, that however much the leaders might quarrel, the colony was thriving. The shouting crowd on the wharf was well if plainly dressed, there were many rosy, healthy children, dancing with excitement, among them. The harvest fields were rich with corn, the orchards heavy with fruit, new and substantial houses had been built. Philadelphia was the garden city of Penn's dream, and Pennsbury Manor, which he had feared neglected, was no more dilapidated than a little attention could repair. Everything needed only the hand of the master to be set again on the right course.

Penn was equal to it. His old energy came back. He could interview the opposing parties, and with his honest friendliness lead them to make peace. He could see where new laws were needed, and old ones to be amended in the light of new needs. He could travel great distances, by river, on horseback or in his coach along the new-made roads, visiting the outlying settlers, conferring with the governors of neighbouring provinces, and feel no more fatigue than when he was young. The dispute with Lord Baltimore had simply died away, and the two men were now on reasonably easy terms with one another.

Some of Penn's happiest days were spent among his old friends, the Indians. They had not forgotten the Great White Chief, and welcomed him as frankly as ever. He was able to make peace between warring tribes, and persuade them to bring their differences to the Council instead of settling them with a tomahawk!

He had hoped to end his days in peace at Pennsbury Manor, but that was not to be.

King William III was at war with France, and because the French held possessions in America which bordered on the English colonies, America too was involved in the war. Pennsylvania was called on to raise an army to fight the French colonists. This was contrary to the Quakers' convictions. They refused to fight. Again Penn was threatened with accusations of treachery, and his province might be taken from him and a governor put in who would not care in the least for the ideals of Pennsylvania.

There was nothing for it but to go back to England and plead the cause of Pennsylvania in person. He was easier in his mind about leaving, since he had found an honest, capable and devoted young man, James Logan, in whose hands he could safely leave his people.

Hannah was not sorry to go. Pennsylvania was beautiful, Philadelphia was a handsome city, but around it was the untamed forest, and she could not quite overcome her fears. She now had a little son, too, and she wanted him brought up in England. And Tishe? She had left her heart in England.

On November 3, 1701, with Hannah, Tishe and baby John, Penn sailed away from Pennsylvania— for the last time. He never saw it again.

13

THROUGH SHADOW TO LIGHT

FROM this time on we see Penn moving as if into a dark forest, where the patches of sunlight grew fewer and fewer, and the tangled trees threw a deeper and deeper shade.

One sunlight patch was the marriage of Tishe to a young Friend, William Aubrey. They must have been attracted to one another before they parted, as the wedding was so quickly arranged! Another was the joy of seeing his two small grandchildren, son and daughter of Bille, who had married very young. And, of course, there was the warm welcome he had from the Friends in England, who rejoiced exceedingly to have him with them again.

The shadows were the threat that hung over his beloved Pennsylvania, owing to the war with France; his tangle of debts, made worse by the schemes of his deceiving steward and family; and his own failing health. He would have liked to settle down peacefully at Warminghurst, but business kept him continually in London, which never suited him.

Another grief began to show itself. His son Bille was turning out more of a cavalier than a Quaker, and not the best kind of cavalier at that. He was careless and gay and irresponsible. His father sent him to Pennsylvania, hoping that responsibility would steady him, but he behaved so badly there that he was sent home in disgrace. Finally, he abandoned the Quakers altogether.

The darkest point was reached when Penn was actually imprisoned for debt. But with the help of Friends his affairs were settled, and he was released. Through all the troubles his loving, faithful Hannah supported him, and the little children born to her were the delight of his old age.

Then came a series of strokes, and he passed into a twilight land of semi-consciousness, until on July 30, 1718, the full light dawned and he passed peacefully into Life.

A sad ending? He had fought a great fight for freedom and justice in England; in Pennsylvania he had planted a great ideal. Men and women living today, here and in America, have inherited the freedom, justice and ideals for which he fought. We owe a great debt to William Penn.